Long Live Phoenixes

Jasmine Farrell

Copyright ©2018 and 2022 Jasmine Farrell
Second edition: June 2022
Originally published November 2018

All rights reserved. No part of this publication may be reproduced, distributed, or transmitted in any form or by any means, including photocopying, recording, or other electronic or mechanical methods, without the prior written permission of the publisher, except in the case of brief quotations embodied in critical reviews and certain other noncommercial uses permitted by copyright law. For permission requests, write to the author, addressed "Attention: Permissions for Long Live Phoenixes," at the email address below:
jasmine@justbreathejasmine.com
ISBN: 978-1-7379460-0-7
www.jasminefarrell.com

DEDICATION

For every unrecognized phoenix…

TABLE OF CONTENTS

ACKNOWLEDGMENTS .... **i**

Phoenix Law #1 .... **1**

Where I Come From 2

Comparisons 5

Stars and Grandma 6

Phoenix Law #2 .... **7**

Oh, Honey, Live 8

Naked Mirrors 9

Phoenix Prayer 10

Silence 12

Acceptance 13

Acceptance II 14

Acceptance III 15

Why I Told Mama 16

Jasmine 17

On Slowing Down 19

Phoenix Law #3 .... **21**

Destiny Rejection 22

Ex-Pessimistic Phoenix 24

On the Days You Reminisce, Phoenix 25

I Over-Accommodated	27
Transformation Thoughts	28
Why I'm Actin Brand New	29
Speak, Phoenix, Speak	30
The Radiance of Your Everything	32
Phoenix Law #4	**35**
Molting Season	36
Overcome	41
Phoenix Grooming: Why I Cut my Hair	42
Unscathed Phoenix	43
Believe in the Dream, Phoenix	44
Flights to Durham	45
Letter to Bennu	46
Phoenix Law #5	**48**
Strive for the Present	49
Walk Steady Phoenix	50
Phoenix Law #6	**51**
Endurance	52
Endometriosis Phoenix	54
September – December Blues	56
Supported Phoenix	57

Phoenix Law #7	**58**
I was Tired	59
When the Past Lover Calls You	62
Home	63
Cutting the Cord	66
Phoenix Law #8	**67**
Love Deeply, Phoenix	68
Romancin' this Phoenix	69
Theresa	70
I Heard Love Before	72
T with Honey in Philly	74
This Time Around	76
Phoenix Law #9	**79**
How Long Will You Write?	80
We Migratin', Phoenixes	82

ACKNOWLEDGMENTS

I would like to thank my support system:

My father for being in my corner, Auntie Momo for guiding me to just live, my friends for keeping me grounded and my partner for allowing me to just be. This book would not have been complete without the experiences I have faced from 2016-2018. Those two years have pulled out courage, self-accountability, confidence and beautiful connections that I will cherish for years. I appreciate the readers who read my draft and gave honest feedback. They have helped me to dig deeper- to reach my fellow phoenixes-from my heart to theirs. I would like to thank my fellow phoenixes for helping me stay focused on completing Long Live Phoenixes and for inspiring me

to   always   strut   with   my   wings   ready   to   soar.

Phoenix Law #1

Burn brightly,
soar high
and
always
remember where you came from.

Where I Come From

I come from Grandma's
New Year's Eve Peas 'n' Rice,
stiff charismatic hair bangs
and
God-mommies who can sang.

I come from pride-
heroes, strength and a few lies.

A lineage of stories that make the authors
of best sellers envious.
The older folk got tales.
Fierce index finger
to punctuate the line,
"I ain't gonna' say it again to you verbally."

I come from passed down traditions
that should have remained
under vintage evening stars.

I come from hefty kisses,
Vaseline saturated lips.

I come from love.

You know, that sweet sticky confusing peace
we always attempt to grab instead of receiving.

I come from love.

Long Live Phoenixes

I come from cook-up rice, ackee and salt fish.
Pholourie, four for 1$
and ritualistic
Monopoly gamin' every other weekend
with aunty and uncle.

I come from playfulness.

Light hearted grins and cumbersome laughter,
spilling over couches with the stench of mauby
and sorrel,
permeating Grandpa's living room.

I come from perseverance.

Hanging on to a thread
but Mama used the very hairs on her head to make sure we
remained hanging-
sometimes,
bending,
shaking,
but,
never falling.
Never losing grip.

I come from grit.

The laced persistence
to place each foot in front of the other
in order to evolve.
Southern dialect, old wise tales
and old school routines.

Warm air, crisp bacon,
tree swingin' in Valley Stream,
scolding hot coffee,
greasy Blue Magic scalp
and reflective pauses.

I come from *raised right*.
"Keep your elbows off the table.
Keep your head held high.
Keep your name clean,
and remember what your parents taught you."

I come from everything I needed
to get where I'm goin'.

That's where I come from.

Comparisons

Sass like Grandma.
Confidence like Daddy.
Stern like Mama.
An elixir of fragrances,
saturated scents of high and lows,
reconstruction,
growth from the roots-
still trying to settle
beneath the earth of
Manning and Cocorite,
Bedstuy and Hackensack.
Talk back like Grandma.
Curious like Daddy.
Mouth like Mama.
Light hearted like Grandpa.
Heavy hearted like childhood.
Strength like young adulthood.
Humor like Grandma.
Gentle hearted like Daddy.
Dominant like Mama.
Wild soul like me.
Uncouth and lady-like like me.
Arrogantly curious and nurturing.
Sensitive and aggressive.
Teachable and open.
Stubborn like wine stains on white carpets.
Fierce switch like Mama.
Persevere like Mama.
Voice like Mama.
Real Jazzy like me.

Stars and Grandma

I've watched stars overcome
the darkness of night and
sleep quietly during the day.
Stars know the elegance
of shining brightly at the right times and playing the background,
just the same.
Stars humble their beauty for
the naked eye and
illuminate in telescopes.
Constellations.
What a story we have to follow,
such role models we have,
but,
never appreciate.
I have watched those stars glisten under my grandmother's
backyard
as,
grown folk spoke stories too big
for a little girl, like myself, to understand.
I soaked up the perplexed words and ate up the,
"Well, Daddy condoned his sons from doing that"
and
"I dun' told ya'!"
and
"I would like to see a black movie."
"The necessity to support one another is vital."
and
"Do it again, I'll cut ya' behind."
Well, I did understand the latter.

Phoenix Law #2

I will no longer breathe in
the lies they have told me.
I will no longer ruminate on
the lies I've told myself.
I will no longer inhale
false perceptions and wonder
why I am asphyxiating on deceit.

Oh, Honey, Live

When society, family and friends
have decided what your purpose
will be-
when they have outlined your
shadow on the pavement and
named it their own:
Remember, your shadow belongs to you.
Your heart isn't powered
by their good will and innocent intentions.
Let me also mention that their opinions can't remedy your
inner chaos.
Oh, Honey, live.
Just live.
Watch the waves and choose on your own time:
When you will swim
and
when you will simply float.
You've built the boat,
now
you,
ride the waves.
You don't have to behave in a sea
that was meant for you to belly flop in-
sometimes.
Oh, Honey, live.
Just live.
Float on.
Swim on.

Naked Mirrors

And so,
I looked into my visual echo,
with enough tears
to flood Seattle for years and said,
"Do better.
You deserve better.
Better is coming."
Firm tranquility
and
ache flooded my insides.
I said it until I believed it.
Until my heart received it.
The mirror never looked so bare.
I looked at the lines,
gawked at the dark circles,
heaved at the various
times I took my true value
and
placed into the hands of shattered beings.
I embraced the new journey
of recovery,
forgiveness and transitions.
The mirror never looked so bare.

Phoenix Prayer

Sun,
kiss my tears
when silence blankets
the noise within.
Remind me,
it's okay to heal
during spontaneous mornings
where I thought
my wake-up
smile meant everything was okay.

Free flowing winds,
slip on in from the window,
infuse my room,
remind me to just breathe.

Easy is never an option
when on the cusp
of my transitions.

Belly,
give Her a yes
when resistance sits
so eloquently on my round belly.

I've always feared change
but,
I've always allowed it.

Long Live Phoenixes

Soul,
remind my ego that purpose
starts with you.

Moon,
hush my fears and confirm
with my being that I was created for this.

Silence

Indulge the silence
like it was your lover
under a blue light at a basement party.
Grip the hips of the noiseless curves,
surrender to the rhythm of stillness.
Your answers are found
in the bass line
of quiet.
Embrace the silence you have been
attempting to fill with everyone's opinions
and tasteless strobe lights.
Go where you could hear your heart
beating a drum, you once played.
Remember who you are.
Go where affirmations grind slow to
serenity and
true love is
rooted within the crevices of the Divine.
Go where the answers
are awaiting your questions
and
the surrounding beings don't faze you.

Acceptance

When I was six,
I'd mix baby powder,
water
and
stolen silver nail polish together.
Called myself making a hardened paste.
I'd smooth the paste around my favorite
toy tea cup and think about my taste
in the finer things like:
unbreakable tea cups,
soft Play-Doh
and secret kisses from her.
We did some secret cootie catching and releasing
in the crevices of a house that reeked
of prayers, love and anointing oil.
I didn't know any better
back then and it seems
I'm back to square one,
and
I knew better back then
like
I know better now.
Except, my kisses are no longer
surreptitious.

Acceptance II

I kiss in front of red doors,
simply be,
my weird thinking patterns,
awkward gawking and strange taste
in the beautiful things in life like:
strong summer winds
making turf wars with
busy Wall Street employees.
Or,
well behaved twist outs
that cause me to buy
that plastic tiara just for the hell of it.

Acceptance III

I was fine before the grooming.
I'm done pleading with a created creator
to make me something I am not.
To bend, twist and shape me into
a mold that appeases
the dogmatic and frightened.
I am done being ashamed for simply being
…me:
A lil' ol' phoenix
who likes to write,
laugh, shimmy
and dance in my room at 3am.

Why I Told Mama

Because,
a woman like that
is too worthy
to be hidden in cupboards.
Too vibrant
to sit in the attic of minds.

Because,
my heart leaps,
pushes against my cheekbones,
just by the thought of her-
I smile.
Her evidence is hidden
on the balls of risen cheeks.

Because,
love peels open closed lips
and
spreads its good news.

…Blame love.

Jasmine

Used to ride the bus of mediocracy.
Childhood wounds
decorated the vehicle
like stubborn stains on mauve
pant suits.
Had a dream Mahdi
told me to get off the bus.
I got off the bus.

Flights to places
that harbor good grass,
light hearted breezes,
and
soda pop
that fizzles on taste buds,
long after it slides down my larynx.

I am worthy to indulge in the little things
that I was told were venomous.

I was born a free-flowing skeptic.
A curious wonderer who
wanders.
I was designed to dance
aimlessly and free.
Flail my arms,
wiggle my hips,
feet to ground-
hands to transparent guitars,
waist riffing to beats,
while air boogies with free hair

and summer dresses
with sass on seams.
I was made to jive.

I was born with
the hunger to voyage-
to discover-
to leap within
then go out with all the love
I could muster,
all the giggles
I carried from past lives.
All the cackles that tickled
underneath my chest,
anticipating to share
free falling
kee-kee's and laughter.

I was born with a free flowing,
curious heart.
I will no longer allow
shelter,
ceilings,
numbers,
aesthetics
and
pain to hinder me.

Nah.

On Slowing Down

Aunty Angelou told us
to cease agonizing over untold stories.
So, I search to speak.
To seek within the silence,
searching for a hum,
a mumble of yearning
so, the words can gurgle in my throat.
I want to discover the choice to
belch out freedom stories
and
unlock the narratives that were
shushed to corners
like,
shame was its inheritance.

I want to find the place where
I first rolled up my tongue,
unthreaded my honey tone
and
etched the words of *me* underneath my skin.
I want to dismantle that place.
I want to heal that moment,
tie it in purple
and
paint it whole.
Unravel it golden
and
affirm my tongue worthy.
I want to search for my untainted lines
in the nothingness,
in sunlit rooms of

color and clustered passion.
I honor the silence.
The empty air.
The heavy wisdom
and
lingering epiphanies that
hang on the ceiling,
next to the crystal chandelier centering.

Grounding makes sense *here*.
Courageously burning brightly in the
chaotic bedlam is okay *here*.
Rising by default happens *here*.
Stripping away the layers is good *here*.
Vulnerability is nestled into the crevices *here*.
It's always okay *here*.
The now.
The peeling of *what was* in the reflecting
silence.
I will find the untold stories
in the now while reflection swings like pendulums
and crisp accountability.

Phoenix Law #3

Stop searching for your voice down the throats of other people. Look within.

Destiny Rejection

The first time you called me
beautiful,
it was too late in the day
to carry any weight.
Something about that tardy sway
of your lips to affirm me,
made me chuckle something stale and eerie.
I no longer craved to hear what
I discovered on my own.
You girdled
your body, mind and spirit to a portrait
my essence threw splatter paint on.
I just wanted to whistle the harmony God gave me
but,
you pressed my lips together
with your thumb and shame finger.
I remember having to hum songs
and
muzzle my own melody,
pleaded to just run towards
innocence's mystery.

My destiny was not written for you.
You do not hold the pen
that overcasts my oak pages.
Your ink will not show here.

My story wasn't written for you.
It's true.
But you have carried a story-
a purpose.

a continuation of your legacy,
the ever-evolving study of perseverance
churning in my veins,
the understanding that I come from
a lineage where strength, wisdom,
rhyme and velvet aggression are wrapped in experiences and stories.
You no longer carry me now.
But you will always be with me.
In my walk, in my stern tones and nurturing agenda.
You are here.

You intended to lead me to a path where harm
was nothing more than southern folklore.
Your agenda was to raise me right
and full of that *good light*.

Metamorphosis lingered since I was 7,
but the heaven you spoke of,
the God you uttered wouldn't allow
this kind of Jasmine.
I get it.

I respect it.
But I've rejected it.
I respectfully reject the destiny
you've written for me.

Ex-Pessimistic Phoenix

Cease expecting the sun to fall into the sea every time you see choppy waters.

On the Days You Reminisce, Phoenix

Sometimes you'll miss the memories of
laughter and inside jokes.

> You don't know what emotionally abusive is.
> You tempt me to show you what it's really like.

And, some days you'll consider rerouting your destination
and fly back to what you've known

> This is what you wanted all along.
> You wanted me to be angry.
> You wanted aggression.
> You want drama.
> This is satisfying to you.
> It's too weird for a man
> to really want to listen and support you.
> You hate me.
> You wanna' see me break.

But, on the days you reminisce and ponder *what ifs*,
remember this:

> Are you afraid of me?
> Am I deceitful?
> or are you a little girl afraid for her life?
> I've never known such a self-obsessed
> cheating individual like you.
> Why are you so pathetic?

Toxicity should never nestle in your feathers.
Keep soaring.

I Over-Accommodated

Lost my voice in crowd.
Placed hand to mouth,
let the masses get loud.
Kissed my hands goodbye
and
surrendered them to zip ties,
pacification and fear of rejection.
Something in my belly kept
churning for my attention.
Too busy preparing to nose dive into distraction.
I forgot what my bass line sounded like.
I could no longer recognize my own
footsteps…

Transformation Thoughts

I sunk my teeth into renewal
like phoenixes to sulfur.
I don't want egg-ling dreams anymore.
I'll return the
fake glow-in-the-dark starfish décor
and wish for genuine.
I will wish upon genuine stars
that my Grandpa pointed at in 1994.
I will adore what my heart yearns for
and not what they ache for me.
No more.

Why I'm Actin Brand New

I didn't want a veil over my voice anymore.

Speak, Phoenix, Speak

I won't place a muzzle over my story for your comfort.
I will no longer mumble my realities that you sprinkle
your theories over,
to make you feel better.
I won't leave a lump in my throat to make
the shaking cease beneath your chest.
Fuck you.
I have a voice too.
And,
underneath the bassline
you so happen
to fetishize,
pass the sultry humming of the syllables I release,
I'm actually
fucking
speaking.

Placing periods
at the beginning of my narrative
will not be permitted here anymore.
Derailing my truths with hopes to shut me up- no more.
This is not a rut I fell in.
This is my narrative.
This is my sashay through hallways,
wanting to bury my presence
because,
I was taught not shine too bright
and
to walk like I reside underneath gravel.
This is my epiphany to transform,
rediscover the sound of my life note.

Long Live Phoenixes

My strength to breathe and heave my screams
of the never-ending,
"will there ever be an ending?" cycle
of familial injustices, desensitized themes
to justify why my kind have
lesser than bodies.
Lesser than beauty.
Lesser than minds.
But…
we're always supposed to be kind.
Always supposed to be meek.
Only part our lips after you speak.
Fuck you.
I won't place a muzzle over my story for your comfort.
I will speak.

The Radiance of Your Everything

There will come a season
when demeaning
the way
your soul shines
will make you shutter
something bleak…

Who told you to hate the radiance of your everything?
To twist your mouth ever so foully at the
way you gracefully move as mortals do?

Close your ears to the broken lips
and well-meaning monsters
closing in on your potential,
desiring to claw at your essence.

Open your heart
to the truth that's always been
present:

The radiance of your everything
shimmers a light,
encompassing the attributes that make
your ancestors proud.
That make your heart wanna' burst into particles
of breathtaking accomplishment.
And,
qualities
that sit limp, lack luster and judged.
That flaw-fully burn ruffled feathers,
that make you wanna' crawl

into a ball and wait
until the blaze passes by.

You are the blaze!

The burning,
the yearning to evolve.
The desire to keep going,
the temperament that isn't
always under wraps,
the blemish on your cheek,
the times you wanna' be strong,
but, instead feel weak.

Love it all.

Embrace the sweeping everything
that brightens up select rooms
and bows out of others.
That trail blaze through the common
and hides in the indifference,
that's dimly lit on somedays
and blaringly bold and bodacious on other days.

Shine.

Embrace those flaws and imperfections
like the sun told you its greatest secret.
Walk fiercely in your unique glow like life
made a tempo to your strengths.

Oh, there will come a season
when you will grow weary

of trying to squeeze in
faux felt affirmations and
the acceptance of yourself
through others.

I hope that season begins today.

Phoenix Law #4

I will no longer allow people to lay their insecurities on my chest like rose petals on Valentine's Day bed spreads.

Molting Season

It's molting season
and
I'm fighting for reasons to keep
the dead feathers
on my thighs,
wings
and feet.
Rubbing, *Used-To-Be* butter on my skin,
hoping the voice within would
smooth out,
moisturize shut,
cease talking-
let me stay in my *what-was,* rut.

It's molting season
and I'm demeaning
my own quintessence for the sake of dead feathers
and
stubborn scratching of an itch
that doesn't have to be there.

I asked for better.
I've prayed to be a soaring phoenix.
To soar high,
pretty,
boldly awkward and bodaciously me.

LONG LIVE PHOENIXES

Hence, it's now burning season,
to watch the flames and melting
connections of who I was
and
who I am to become.

Phoenix
Phoenix
opened her eyes during the midnight hour.
A settled hush of newness
brushed her being
and
her chest rose.
Shook off the excess ash
as she got up from the apocalyptic pit.
She got up.
Wiggled the creepy crawlers
of toxic connections from her shins
and
grinned at the darkened freedom
she found at the bottom.
She looked up.
Greeted by a speckled prism,
a pearl moon.
She looked up.

Phoenix
released the sacred commentaries
she took heed to until
she eventually,
ceased flying
and
withered away.
Let those commentators
burn her up and blame her
for being such a bold flame.

Long Live Phoenixes

Rise, Phoenix, Rise.
Those aren't heavy weights
on your shoulders.
Those are
Wings, Phoenix, Wings!
Leave it all behind
and
Fly, Phoenix, Fly.

Second Chance
When you rise again
this time,
make sure you bring yourself with you-
no one else.

Overcome

You ain't dead yet.
Rise out of the water
they pushed you in-
yet somehow declared it as
self-drowning.
Overcome.
Rise.
With water sittin' steady in your lungs,
with murky water sticking to your feathers,
rise.
Overcome.

Phoenix Grooming:
Why I Cut my Hair

Because,
one morning,
I woke up tired of being scared.
Tired of believing
that I'd meet the grim reaper
at the bottom of my soul.
Weary of thinking that
I'd die from what I'd discover
at the gate of my quintessence.
Because,
I had falling out with fear,
a letting go of withering traditions.
A dismantling of core bad habits.
An awaited annihilation of what was
and what is.
I am lighter.
I am thinking higher.
I am learning again.
Discovering more.
Plus, it's fly on me.

Unscathed Phoenix

Some Phoenixes
haven't seen their wings
conflagrate in mid-air,
while watching their goals
pull away from them
as they crash down.
They're unaware of their
platinum-power-play-resurrection.
Rebirth breath and rejuvenated giggles,
are simply jargon for unscathed phoenixes.
The *un-reborn* Phoenix.
The *never-seen-persecution* Phoenix
Oh, the day they realize
what it's like to rustle and rattle
through their own ashes and cracked eggshells.
Oh, the day they realize how high they'll
soar once they've had their wings scorn and torn…
Only to be reborn again…

Believe in the Dream, Phoenix

We tie our dreams to pessimism
then wonder why our dreams don't
soar like,
 straight outta' the ashes Phoenixes.
Believe in those wings.
Release the strings of old ways
and comfy restrictions.

Flights to Durham

Watching clouds below me,
my heart chuckles at the nonsensical vows
I told my soul.
Like,
never leaving my comfort zone
or
pushing away golden hearts who merely
wanna' love my essence
for what it was,
what it is,
and what it will be.

Letter to Bennu

Congeal my thoughts
to the truth my soul's been speakin'
during the quiet moments of 3am.
Slumber once knew the sight
of my kissing eyelids until an awakening
slipped through my controlled meditations.
Spirit is irrepressible, they say.
Encompassing my stubborn,
pulling at my pride,
confronting childhood traditions,
long lived mindsets.
The chest of my transformation
heaves at the dewy shifts
and I want to run, Bennu.
I want to run.

Molting season makes my mind
shiver something relieving
but,
I hesitate at the mystery
as vile perceptions slide from my eyelids-
teardrops, I guess.

If I surrender, will the rumbling
within my wings cease?
Will my soul feel elated as peace
reunites with the borderline of my quintessence?

Or will I be burned again?
Will I be burned?
Just…

LONG LIVE PHOENIXES

Congeal my thoughts
to the truth my soul's been speakin'.
Maybe, then, I'll trust the process.

Let trust of the unknown rise
like you did the Nile.
Let it rise, Bennu.

Phoenix Law #5

Walk like you've never knew of shame.

Strive for the Present

Sometimes,
survival busyness
bites us in the ass-
during the mornings we believe
the sun is that teacher
we authentically hated
and
the feelings were mutual.
Strive to be present anyway.
Wiggle your beak,
shimmy your wings
and soar anyway.

Walk Steady Phoenix

Said you knew your value
and
the weight of your feathers now.
Shed off the redundancy
and excess dreams of what
they wanted you to be.

You held tight to your dreams.
Hid your visions at the seams of your
colored wings-
your red and orange.

Let them loose.
Set them free.
Let them flow with your journey.
Strut fiercely and wipe off the negativity.

Phoenix Law #6

Don't let the scars cease your fire.

Endurance

Sometimes,
your light will get dim.
Sometimes,
tears are the solution.
Keep flying.
Allow the thorns to ignite new flames.
Strength is found in your blaze.
Exquisiteness is buried beneath your pain.
Endurance sticks to your feathers during winter seasons
and your chest is quaking from this world's promising chill.
Cry, soar low, cease speaking for a while,
bellow in pillows during witching hours.
But, don't let the scars cease your fire.

Departed Phoenix
Unaware of your existence,
until your corpse passed through.
Too late to feel you-
just in time for your death.
Side effects of a sassy endometrium.
Torn over what unknowingly
existed due to a known resistance.
Unseen egg-ling.
A little relieved.
I never knew of your silence.
Your absence was so flamboyant.
Red streaks on porcelain.
I denied your hints.
Endometriosis leaves water marked prints on reality checks.
It was pay day on May 8th, 2017

Endometriosis Phoenix

A year ago,
I was positive that the stars were broken.
I wished upon constellations
to pull away thorns from left ovary,
clear away
unseen symptoms,
unforeseen aches at open mics
and theatre shows,
unnecessary bail outs of
"normal reproduction."
Is my womanhood defined here?
Were those really stars I was wishing upon
or
was it just hospital lights,
blurred out
from tears of confusion and misconstrued thoughts?
Endo-belly birthing
cancelled dates, sick days and M.I.As.
Absent memories with loved ones
as a twin bed held a body with unrelenting pain.
"But you don't look sick."
A cyclical line that slid from
tone-deafened lips
that wrapped around my mind
and abdomen.
I still look for answers on the internet
and in between the pauses of a doctor's reply to my inquires.
I still rub my belly under constellations.
I still walk though.

LONG LIVE PHOENIXES

I still smile in between the aches
and give gratitude a head nod.
I'm finna' be just fine.

September – December Blues

Usually,
I let the pen ink speak for me.
Release my pain on dead oak trees
and surrender to the silence.
I let it go.
Dive towards better moments and kiss progress in the rain.
But sometimes,
I vent on my flesh,
hold my thoughts hostage.
My mystery isn't sexy in these parts.
My silence isn't reflective in this place.
It's a kidnapping of my voice.
A robbery gone wrong and I've seemed to have lost my hands to reach out.
The word, "Help" dangles from my tongue
but,
my mouth refuses to set it free.
Sometimes,
I feel as though winter settling in my chest
is the best idea
and I fight to procrastinate executing that idea….
I lose some battles, Suga.
but I get the peroxide
and partner up with ambition to win the war.

Supported Phoenix

On the days we thought
he/she would fix his/her lips to swallow the sun,
swallow the blood of our fallen heroes
and whisper into the heart of their corpses,
"Hope is a myth."
Let's remember our darkest days
and how we called out to the sun
as if our grandparents were behind us
and our ancestors were holding our feet up for a boost.
We will rise out of this.

Phoenix Law #7

No one has the power to
determine your worth,
to make you curtsy at
mediocracy,
to determine how high, you can
soar-
unless you give it to them.

I was Tired

In the end,
I was drained.
Stained with resentment,
relief and reassurance to leave.
I felt the weight of us lift
from my shoulders
and I shimmied something
unruly yet,
right.

In the end,
I reflected truthfully.
My eyes half full of tears,
yet,
I never leaked a drop.
Just a simple sigh of grief,
I reflected truthfully.

You smeared your projections on my skin
like   coconut   oil   after   evening   showers.
Splattered your insecurities on the dress
I allowed God to heal,
and self-love that
I embroidered on the seams.

I found the lessons in this hidden blessing.
I learned not to sew my garment
with people who don't know
their own thread colors.
I learned that I don't
like large amounts of hypocrisy.

Throwing Bounty towels at my mess
won't make yours go away any sooner.

In the end
I was tired.
Lifted you up when you were down,
affirmed you when it appeared your soul
would sink to middle of the earth.

You were always so hard on yourself,
just like I was,
and hefty self-loathing lovers are
no match made in heaven-
neither is it hell.
It's not balanced.
It's an uncertainty.
It is stagnant pressure,
a stifling passion that appears like an anchor.

You'd rather fall into a sink hole of self-pity
than to take responsibility of your actions.
We weren't walking toward reconciliation.
This is not a situation to run back to.
It was a falling out and
I fell smack dab into freedom.

In the end,
I was tired.
Tired of waiting.
Waiting for you to see me.
To hear my voice telling you the secrets of what makes
my heart do somersaults.
I am not perfect.

Long Live Phoenixes

I never pretended to be.
You threw stones on my road to self-discovery
and called me selfish when not allowing
you to overtake my essence.
In the end,

I

    Was

        Tired.

When the Past Lover Calls You

When the past lover who discouraged you
from flying above
your over cautious ego that rolled like thunder-
you know,
the one who minimized your efforts
to soar over
destructive thoughts that snowed
in your higher self's
signal to engage within?
Yeah, that one.
When he/she calls you during their winter storms
it's because they've realized
just how cold the world can be without you.
Don't look back.
You're better off.
Keep flappin', soarin', and allowin' fresh wind
to slide through your feathers.

Home

One day,
I met you on 34th street and 8th avenue.
I was craving for your presence
and you hungered for mine.
Time showed us we were merely comfort
food to each other.
Heavy bites to clogged arteries and common sense.
Relentless wrenching of my foundation.
You attempted to build a home out of me
when there was one already present.

Well…
I left my own home of
dignity, peace and Grandma's good wisdom
to go gallivanting down streets my gut
told me to give no second glance.
I went gallivanting down blocks
I've seen friends have their teeth and peace
knocked out of.
Their dreams
now fertilize the lawns of lack luster
companions.

One day,
I met you on 34th Street and 8th avenue.
Looked into your eyes
and
called you home.
Yet, it appears
love never paid me a visit.
I'd send words of encouragement in a bouquet of reassurance,

yet love never
responded to me.
I reached out in poems.
Shrunk my radiance for it.
Let go of my essence for it.
Dusted the beautiful relics in the living room and
ignored the foreign hands trying to gloss your lips.

Infatuation, manipulation and quiet skeletons
nailed the floor boards down.
You'd tell me there were no nails
as the screws
pricked the bottom of my feet with each step.
The windows were always foggy,
I was always cleaning out that
damn drain.
With your rose-colored glasses
and that roundabout gate to cover your pain,
you never saw the mess.
Never addressed the mosquitoes biting my legs in the kitchen.
You'd just sit on the couch and lotion yourself
in gloss and regurgitated words.
You said
I was what you were looking
for,
as I stood there,
watched you pluck my feathers
and
hush my dignity to the corners of the attic
thinking-
maybe, I was just *too much*.
I'd stand up for myself,
you called me self-centered.

Long Live Phoenixes

Pulled the rug from underneath me
when I called you out on your bullshit.
I let you burn me...
Set my quintessence a blaze.
Let the embers snow in every inch of our bedroom.
Luckily,
you never cared too much to know me.
I am Phoenix, baby.
So, as I rose out of my ashes and pushed through molting season.
I ceased cleaning.
Ignored the floor boards,
ceased arguing to be seen at eye level
and strut out the door.

I used to look into your eyes
and call you home,
yet it appears
love never paid me a visit.
I'd send words of encouragement in a bouquet of reassurance
yet,
love never
responded to me.
Infatuation, manipulation and quiet skeletons
nailed the floor boards down.
You had the nerve to ridicule
my naked strength to leave home and
visit love for myself.
How dare you.

Cutting the Cord

I think I made the right choice.
You know,
to cut the cord that draped
around my neck
like lavender lace on Easter.
Sun shined brightly on such
suffocation.
Oh, how it shined.
and
oh, how they smiled
at the beautiful rope
that festered discreetly,
strand by strand.
Oh, how they smiled sweetly.
Neatly crossed their arms
at such a glazed porcelain romance.
You were a neck shackle,
dipped in gold
jangling, clanking, minimizing,
pulling me into the
sink hole you sank in with such pride.
I surrendered to the heaviness
I did not heave.
I did not fight it.
I did not scream.
I did not flinch.
For I was so sure I was sinking
to the other side
of the earth where beauty and true love
wasn't as complicated as you made it.

Phoenix Law #8

Let love in as if X
commanded it
from his living room.
You'll fly higher.

Love Deeply, Phoenix

And,
when you are loving him/her
from here to the moon,
make sure you are loving yourself
from here
to the core
of the andromeda galaxy.

Romancin' this Phoenix

Rub my booty
and
buy me crystals.
Tickle my stern persona
until I get the giggles.
Give me big autumn leaves from Central Park
and
tell me your secrets after dark.
Peel my defensive switch
from the sides of my little hips.
When I lose sight of my dreams,
ask me why I don't take my wings
seriously.

Theresa

I met a woman
who enticed my passion
to rise like phoenix fire.
Shook my radiance,
from its slumber,
by the shoulders
and asked,
"When was it last fed?"

What powerful energy she has.

To uneventfully sit
and make dormant gifts
wake up from forced slumbers
and a forgotten comatose.
Bare and scared,
my poetry found warmth and courage
after months of manipulation
and asphyxiation,
chained to its ankles.

I met a woman who settles fear at the root
and
makes my anxiety bow in silence.
Does she catch rain with her bare hands
and
hydrate Jasmine petals?

Her tales hold wisdom captive
and kiss my attention like
Grandmas to bedtime kiddies.

Long Live Phoenixes

She's worth never letting go
until my chest quits to rise and fall
in a Bengay-smelling-room.

She's the hero who reminds us,
we are our own heroes.

The backbone in my dreams.
The tap dancer on my nerves.
The hefty laughter in my joy.
The sashay in my dramatic antics.

I finally met someone
who sets my soul on fire
and the flames never burn
and anguish doesn't become of it.

Have I fallen for a fellow Phoenix?

Timeless wisdom from her lips.
Has she risen from her ashes various times?
Peace, synchronicity and evolution
crackle and spark.
Evidence of growth in the forever blaze.
I'm amazed at how nonchalantly she lays
after telling the world fuck you to its rules.

I met a woman who I desire to intertwine
my heat with during quick mornings and long nights.
I met a woman who has startled my life
in the most harmonious way
and
I hope we blaze mellifluously for as long as Phoenixes can live…

I Heard Love Before

Love sounds like you when you laugh.

Late to T
You were my cup of tea from the beginning.
But,
I was too busy drinkin' poison to take a sip of you.
Your sensual tongue,
intriguing words.
enticing mind,
and notable brown sight.
Soft lips.
Thick hips.
Thick legs I could gawk at
way after Armageddon.
Lordt…

T with Honey in Philly

A high I abhorred coming down from.
A ride I adored cummin' down on.
Vulgarity on my lips,
your shoulders harbor pressed fingertips.
Lick hips like sugar.
Rub this clit of mine-
honey drips.
Stir in passion.
Vibrational exchange as I change rhythm,
with every bounce,
your spirit breaks down my deep rumination's algorithms.

My moans be your confirmation.
My squeeze be your reassurance.
Our closeness be my aphrodisiac,
Your thickness be my cup-
heat it up.
Past connections have no relevance
to the ecstasy you pull me in,
to the ecstasy I ride on,
to the vulnerability you slide in-
I give in to you.

Fondle past things you said
in my head,
while another climax comes.
Gripping your shoulders tight
I bite into whispers of surrender
"Yes."
No contender to how you make me feel,
to how you reel me in,

got me feelin' you deep within my stomach.
Chest trembling,
pressure increasing,
I'm clenchin' for control,
but long and behold,
this dripping honey has told it all...

This Time Around

I know how to pick up the pieces.
Gather up shattered images of
joined lips and obnoxious laughter.
I know how to keep going,
even if it means crawling until
I remember how to walk,
like I've
never felt the weight of heartbreak so bad,
it slammed me to my knees.

But, I'd rather not this time.
I want us to fix the portrait of us
like puzzle pieces
then,
make new memories,
conquer new obstacles,
thrive through new storms together
and laugh.
Laugh like we never felt frightened
of losing each other.
Caress each other like we were never in
situations where we almost lost each other.

With You
Morning conversations bathes
the sunrise grogginess.
Rejuvenation is found in your voice.
Time slows down
whenever I whisper your name
amongst mundane rituals.
Just one syllable,
tongue to cheek,
I savor it
like salt water taffy Deon used to give me.
I think about the taste of you...

What do you taste like?
Sugar, sunshine and grit I bet.
A little brown sugar with a hint of lemon, I guess.

I sometimes wish my secrets could lay on your chest.
Undress my silence and responsive, "mmm" in front of you.

Will you hold my tarnished parts and not be moved?
Will you be still as I engrave my fears into the grave?
Will you run when old memories haunt my future actions
and attempt to summon ghostly fears?

For the first time I am scared of losing a partner.
If I do, I'll be okay,
but,
your name will simmer under my belly,
your smile will be a portrait
in my dreams like Monet to impressionism.
I'm petrified of ever having to get over you.
I wanna' be under you.

Your skin tickling mine
your fingers tracing my spine.
Your beautiful big brown eyes swimming towards mine.
You and I disobeying the rules of time.
The sand in the hourglass twisters in the same position.

Listen...
I wanna' be a part of the stories you tell.
I wanna' settle the rumbling in the center of your chest
when you're rushing in the morning.
I wanna' sigh softly under the navy-blue palette
while cacklin' at our dramatic antics and vintage jokes.
I wanna' chase away toxic beliefs with you.
Embrace the changes with you.
Shed away our egos and walk in our higher selves with you.
I wanna' live out loud love with you.
Lavishly uplift each other's energies without tainted agendas.
I wanna' shed away fears with you.
Tell you I'm in love with you and
show you how deep I'm in it, with you.
Be a part of the various journeys that are intertwined
in NYC's melting pot
and feed our voices to those
who know of this beautiful impediment
but,
can't seem to find the words to say it-
with you.

Phoenix Law #9

Let purpose drip from your feathers and faith gloss your beak.
Peace will be found in the chaos of life.

How Long Will You Write?

I will bleed black ink on dead
trees
until all the weeds,
I desired to keep,
leave my fingertips and onto freedom papers.
Until the vines cease the asphyxiation that I allowed.
Until I relinquish the compound leaf
that lost its midrib,
once dignity leaked out of the petiole.
Until I'm no longer ashamed
of the joy I feel when passing rustling
greens, yellows and auburns.
Until the internal ballyhoo of my haiku's,
clinging to the roots of feather pens,
finally
holler something naked and bold.
Until I'm restored, full, set free
and
full willow-treeing in my phoenix skin.
Until my hands shake and my skin wrinkles
something wise
and
ready for old time slumberin'.
Until my eyes are tired of watering new plants
and seeing new stories to tell.
Until my heart decides to retire
and my soul yearns for a new beginning,
I will bleed black ink on freedom papers.

For my Sloppy Souled Phoenixes
On the days when sloppy souls,
such as my own,
have heavy hearts
and overly anxious ruminations that clutter
searching eyes and conditional optimistic minds:
It's best we lay our pretend worries to the clouds.
We tell the *what if* fears to fall under
fine print of how things used to be.
We will look back at page 4
When we've already laughed at how we overcame chapter 7.
We are passed that.
Over the hang-ups and the times
we should have put it up ourselves.
The present is sweet or productive, I'm sure.
Our dreams are waiting to be nurtured, fed and catered too.
Use the strength from within, carry that heavy heart
and keep moving.

We Migratin', Phoenixes

From victim to victor.
Shadows to sunny Sundays.
We movin'.
From desperation
to surrendering.
From poverty consciousness
to
prosperity consciousness.
Migrating to the evolution of us.
Going up north to what is ours.
Leavin' south from what no longer serves us.
Packing up our gifts, goals, phoenix laws and manners-
We ret' to go!
We're movin' up north to abundance.
Time to level up.
Time to prepare,
to soar
for the long haul.
We permanently migratin'
to the place where
fear is just a pinched thought
and
courage drenches our wings
like cloud bursts in May.
We migratin', Phoenixes.

Long Live Phoenixes
Rising from the skeletal,
"When I was little"
fears
and becoming the,
"the best me."
since I was twenty-five.
With endurance glossed wings
and a blaze that can sear katana swords
on the face of my enemies:
I got a long way to go.

We are scintillating.

Long Live Phoenixes,
piercing through
the skies we were given.
Soaring through platters of nimbostratus
and a navy-blue palette.

Hope looks good on us.

We've found our wings,
know how to fly,
just gotta' choose a direction.

Long Live Phoenixes,
we found
our destiny on the ground-
they pushed it off our nest.
We dove down and got it.
Shimmied out of our dove costumes they dressed us in,
we dove down and got it.

No one can dress a destiny on us.

Long Live Phoenixes,
it ain't over yet.
We just found out
that our limits
were hand delivered,
set on our throats like thanksgiving spreads,
We will not swallow stories written for us.
We will not chew on destinies other than our own.

ABOUT THE AUTHOR

Jasmine Farrell is from Brooklyn, NY and internal rhyming is her favorite poetic device. She is a proud late bloomer in *"Being true to oneself."* She has previously published two poetry collections, *My Quintessence* (2014) and Phoenixes Groomed as Genesis Doves (2016). PGAGD was inspired by major life transitions right after her college career. Those two years had her questioning "truths" which shuttered her true self from the world. After a tumultuous and enlightening journey, she learned to look at the world with new eyes. She is committed to using her personal experiences to inspire those on a similar path. She has a few unicorns too.

Check her out online:

Personal Website
http://www.jasminefarrell.com

Social Media
Instagram: @Justbreathejasmine
Twitter: @Justbreathejas

www.ingramcontent.com/pod-product-compliance
Lightning Source LLC
Chambersburg PA
CBHW030043100526
44590CB00011B/311